CHESS FOR KIDS

MY FIRST BOOK TO LEARN HOW TO PLAY AND WIN

CARLA LEE

INDEX

Learning chess is great because:

1. It incentivizes creativity and imagination

It has been proven by a scientific study that by analyzing different possible plays, both of the brain hemispheres work together. These results were valid for expert players as much for amateur ones.

When thinking about possible moves, it's not just about following patterns or repeating previous plays, but evaluating the current possibilities and imagining what could happen until the end of the game.

2. Help kids to understand that their actions have consequences

There are multiple benefits from playing chess for people of all ages and <u>there are specific benefits for children</u>. One of them is that it helps them to accept rules and assuming the consequences of their actions.

It is a game where chances don't play a role. Everything is on the table in plain sight and the movements depend only on the players. There isn't an outside element that could affect the development of the game.

3. **It is entertaining and it improves your mood.**

Let's not forget that chess is still a game, so of course it has the same positive characteristics than any other game.

It is entertaining and allows you to interact with other people, no matter the age or nationality (there is no need to speak another language). You can also play from a distance using several available websites. And it is free or almost free, you just need the board and the pieces or an internet connection.

4. **It improves reading skills**

Finally, another important benefit that chess brings is that it helps children improve their reading skills. In fact, a scientific study found that students who play chess improved their reading skills much more than another group that did not participate in any chess program.

1. PIECES

PAWN

- Each player has 8 pawns.
- They are placed on the second row.
- They are placed along the entire second row, as can be seen in the image.

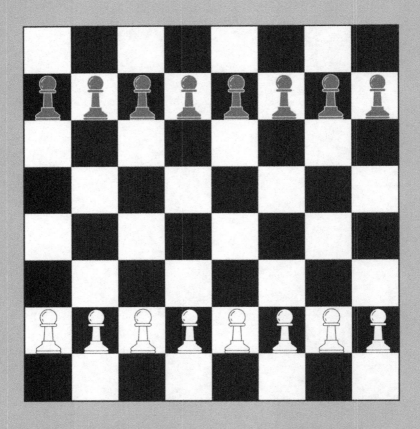

ROOK

- **Each player has 2 rooks.**

- **They are placed in the first row, one in each corner as shown in the image.**

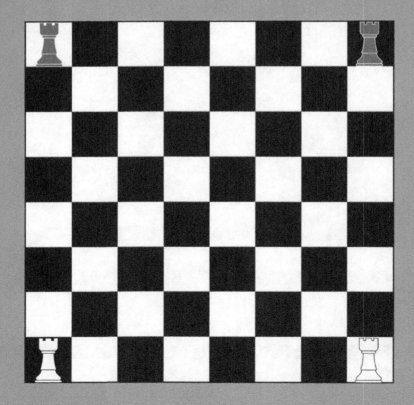

KNIGHT

- **Each player has 2 knights.**

- **They are placed on the first row.**

- **Each knight is placed between the rook and the bishop.**

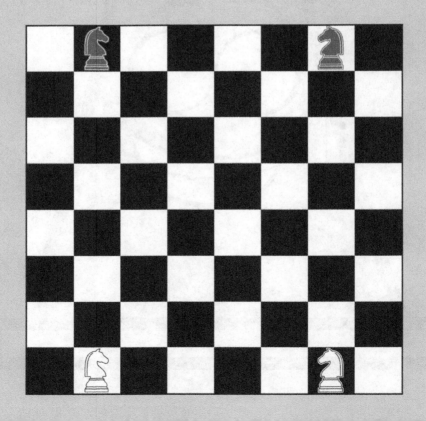

BISHOP

- **Each player has 2 bishops.**

- **They are placed on the first row.**

- **You have to place one between the knight and the queen and another between the king and the knight.**

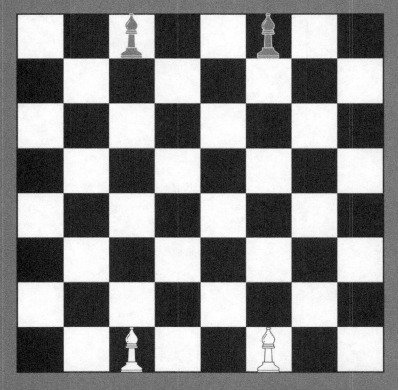

QUEEN

- **Each player has 1 queen.**
- **It is placed on the first row.**
- **The queen is placed between the bishop and the king.**

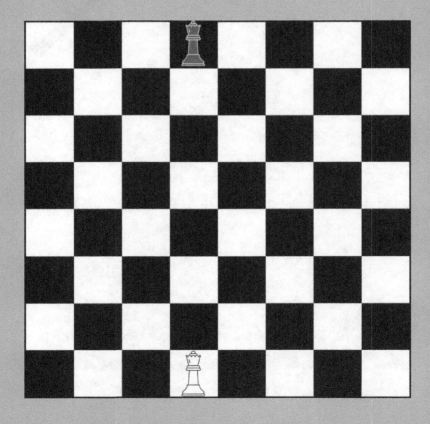

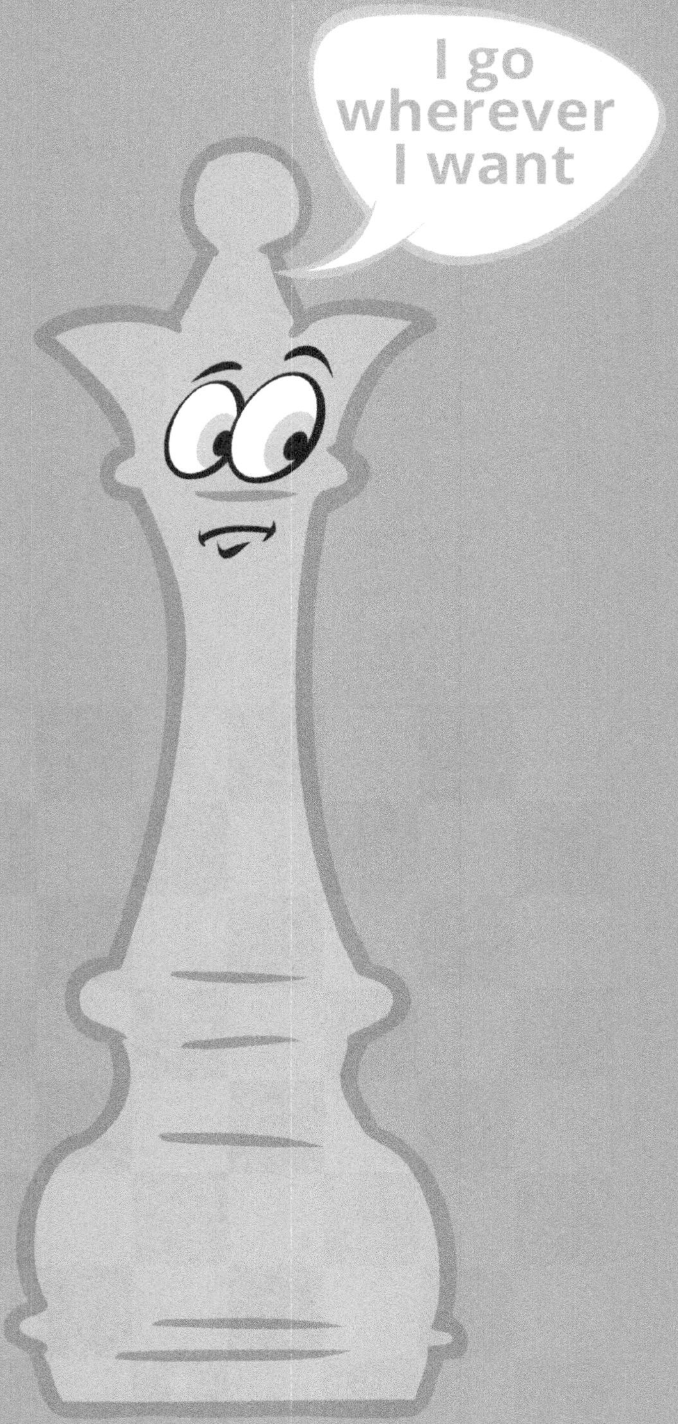
I go wherever I want

KING

- **Each player has 1 king.**

- **It is placed on the first row.**

- **It is placed between the queen and the bishop.**

2. How to move the pieces

- PAWN
- ROOK
- BISHOP
- KNIGHT
- QUEEN
- KING

PAWN

- Yellow dots show the possible moves which a pawn can make from its current position.
- It moves forward just one square at a time.
- On its first move, it can move up to two squares forward.
- It can't go backwards.
- It can take a rival's piece if it is on a diagonal square in front of the pawn as you can see in the picture (the white pawn could capture the black pawn piece). It can't move to a diagonal square if it's empty.
- It has two special moves: promotion and passant.

ROOK

- Yellow dots show the possible moves which a rook can make from its current position.
- It can move as much as you want across the board.
- It can move only one direction at a time.
- It can only move by rows, horizontal or vertical (not diagonally).

KNIGHT

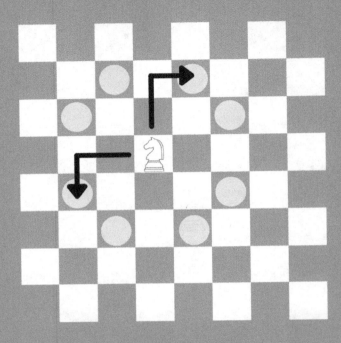

- Yellow dots show the possible moves which a knight can make from its current position.
- It moves like an "L": 2 horizontal or vertical squares and 1 perpendicular square.
- The move ends on a different color than the one at the beginning.
- It can jump on top of whichever piece (your own or your rivals) in order to finish its move.
- You can capture a piece if it is placed on the last square where the knight goes.

BISHOP

- Yellow dots show the possible moves which a bishop can make from its current position.
- It moves diagonally, either on the white squares or on the black squares.
- It can move as many squares as you like in one turn.
- It can only move once per turn.

QUEEN

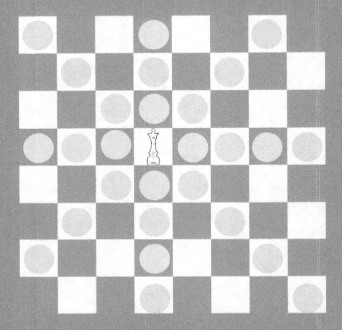

- Yellow dots show the possible moves which a queen can make from its current position.
- It can move horizontal, vertical and diagonally, but only one direction at a time per turn.
- It can move as many squares as you like at a time.

KING

- Yellow dots show the possible moves which a king can make from its current position.
- It can move in all directions, but one square at a time.
- It can't take a piece if there is another one defending it.
- Its special move is "Castling", on which the king moves to the side of the rook, only if it is its first move and the square is vacant and not threatened by the rival.
- A king can't checkmate another king.

3. Elements

King	Queen	Rook	Bishop	Knight	Pawn

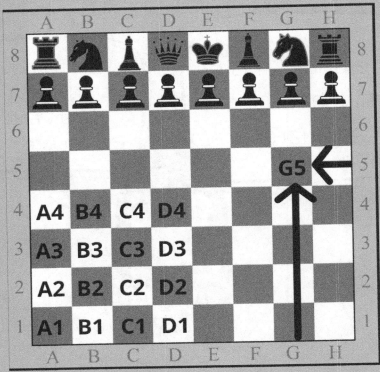

The positions of each square are called "**Algebraic notation**"

4. Special moves

CASTLING

It is a special move in which the king and the rook move at the same time.

You can only use Castling if:

- **The king and the rook haven't moved at all.**

- **There is no piece between the king and the rook.**

- **The king is not on check.**

- **At the end of the move, the king doesn't end up on a square threatened by an opponent's piece.**

Short castling

The king moves 2 squares to the right and the right rook moves 2 squares to the left as you can see shown on the picture.

Long castling

The left rook moves 3 squares to the right and the king moves 2 squares to the left, as you can see shown on the picture.

PASSANT

If a pawn, in its first move, moves 2 squares forward and ends up next to a rival's pawn, this rival pawn can capture it, as if it has only moved one square. The winner pawn would have to take place on the diagonal square.

This is a move that's only valid if it's played right after the pawn has moved the two squares forward.

PROMOTION

If the pawn moves across the board up to the other end, then that piece can be promoted to a better one with greater value and power.

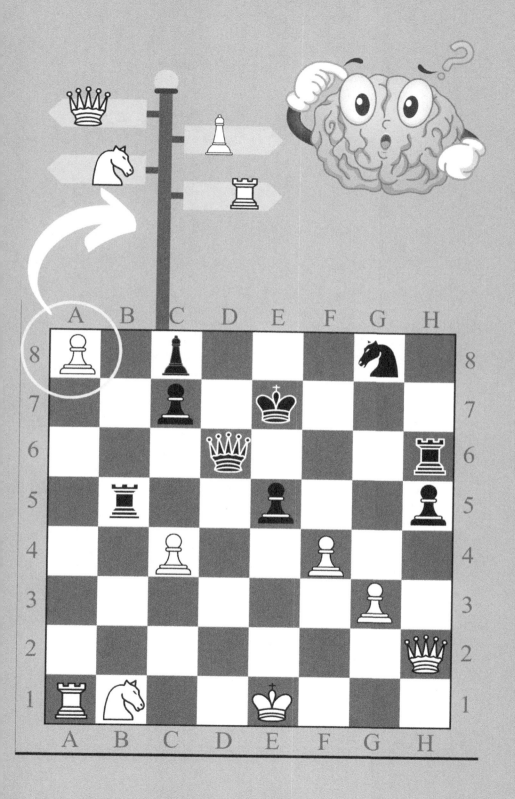

CHECK

Check is when the king or queen of one of the players is threatened to be captured on the next turn by a rival's piece.

If there is no way out for the king piece, then it's a Checkmate and the game is over. Some of the ways to get out of a "Check" are:

- Move the king to a non threatened square.
- Capture the piece the king is threatened by.
- Block the check by placing another piece in between.

Possibles ways out of a Check

Checkmate example

5. Some rules

- The player with white pieces goes first.

- No piece can jump over other pieces except the knight.

- Each player can only move one piece at a time. "Castling" move is an exception.

- If there is a square occupied by your own piece, it can't be replaced by another one of our pieces. It is only possible to occupy a square where our rival has a piece on it, which is better known as "capturing or taking" the piece.

The king can't be captured. If the king is threatened to be captured on the next turn, it's called a "check" and the king at risk must protect itself on its next move or be protected by another piece. If this is not a possibility, then it is checkmate and the owner of the threatened king loses the game.

- All pieces can move backwards except pawns.

- Every player must move a piece on their turn to play.

6. End of game

a) Checkmate

Unlike the rest of the pieces, the king is the only one that can't be captured. If the rival can take the king on the next turn and there is no way out, then the game is over.

b) Quitting the game

Any player could quit the game at any point, so the winner would be the opponent who doesn't quit.

c) <u>Draw or tie</u>

The game can end as a draw or tie under these conditions:

- If none of the kings is in check but both players don't have any possible move available for next turn, the case is called "drowned king".

- If neither player can't get to a checkmate position due to the nature of the remaining pieces. For example: king vs king, king vs king and bishop, king vs king and knight, king and bishop vs king and bishop.

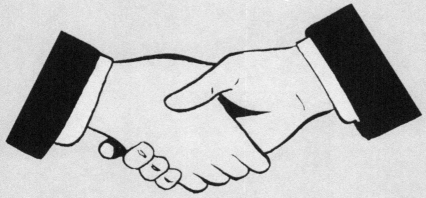

- If the players agree to Draw.

d) Waste of time

If the game is played under time conditions, the game could end when one of the players uses all the time he/she has. Players can have a certain amount of time or a number of moves they can make on a certain term.

7. The Sicilian Defense

The Sicilian Defense is the most common choice for brave players who are playing with the black pieces.

It is very easy, if the player using whites on the first move uses e2 pawn to e4, then the player using blacks could move the c7 pawn up to c5.

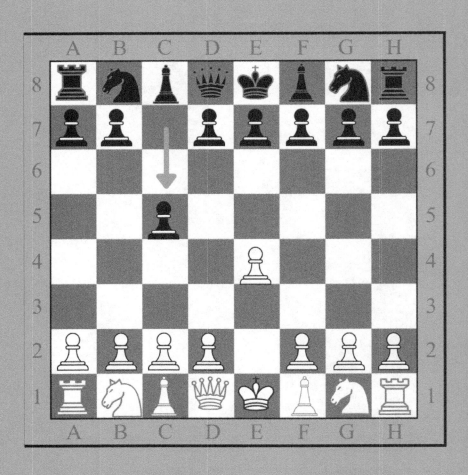

On most chess games, whites play on the first move the pawn to e4, then the knight to f3 and later the pawn to d4. This is done to conquer the central space on the board.

So if blacks, on their first move after e4, place the pawn on c5, it changes everything and whites will be forced to change their strategy by having to move another piece.

8. The French Defense

The French Defense is one of the first strategic openings every chess player must learn to win.

If you are playing blacks, and whites decide their first move to be e4, then as blacks, you could open by moving your e7 pawn up to e6.

As blacks, on your second move, you could move your d7 pawn up to d5 just because you would be already protected enough in order to move forward.

If the whites take your d5 pawn after, then your d6 pawn will be ready to take that piece on the next move.

You should be aware that by doing this opening, then your c8 Bishop would be harder to move, so think carefully.

9. The Slav Defense

The **Slav Defense** is an opening for blacks to defend the d5 pawn with the c7 pawn.

This is a usual response if whites move their pawns to d4 and c4 squares (known as Queen's Gambit).

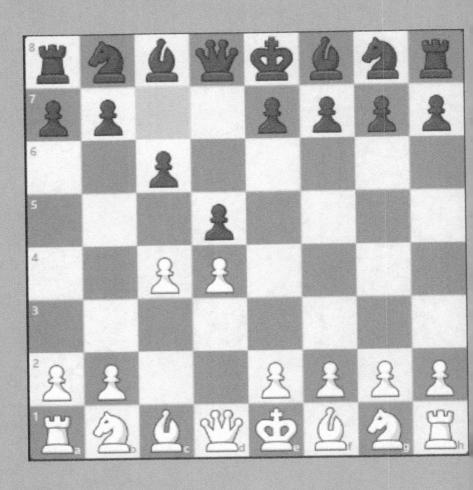

The Slav Defense is an opening developed by great players from Slavic countries and right now it's very trendy as a response to Queen's Gambit move.

This move creates an impenetrable wall for blacks, too tough to crack by whites.

After this, you could move the e7 pawn up to e6, this way you would be creating a pawn chain. Be aware that your c8 Bishop will be trapped by doing these moves.

10. The Italian Game

The Italian game consists on opening space for the queen and the bishop by moving the pawn e2.

Steps:

1. **Move the pawn e2 two spaces forward. While playing blacks, move e7.**
2. **Move your knight to f3 (next possible move for knight is to catch e5 black pawn). Playing blacks, move knight to c6 (if a piece catches e5 pawn, your knight would catch it on the next move).**
3. **Attack: Move your bishop to c4.**

These three steps can be done by whites or blacks and don't depend on your oponent moves. Remember you are playing this to make room for the bishop and queen.

After this you can do several moves, like:

- Protect your king: Castle on your next move (this move is explained on chapter 2)
- The white bishop is threatening some black piece to be promoted, and first you would have to take f7 pawn. Maybe you could move twice the f3 Knight to catch f7 pawn.

Do whatever you want depending on the choices made by the other player. Always keep calm and think about your next three moves.

#FF84D0

11. The Ruy-Lopez

The Ruy Lopez opening is like the Italian game but placing the white bishop on B5.

It has the same purpose, to open up space for castling, to create enough space for the queen and bishop to move and also to put preasure on the center black pawns so that they are forced to move forward.

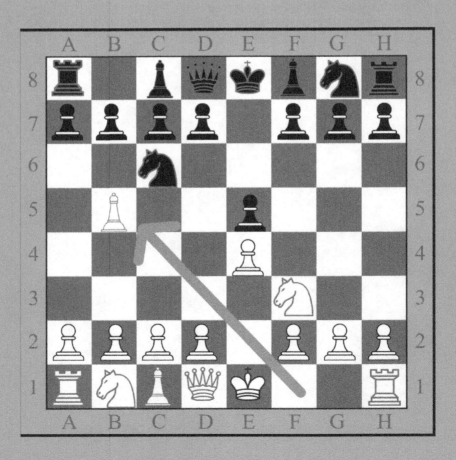

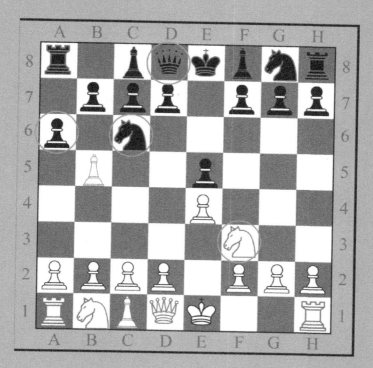

If you were the blacks:

- You could move your a7 pawn to a6 to make whites decide to take your black knight.
- After this, you can take white bishop with one of your pawns.
- Be careful, as the play after that, is usually the knight taking your e5 pawn.

As blacks, you could move your queen to e7 or g5.

This is all for now...

If you liked it, please, leave me a review on the website where you bought it, it just will take you a minute or less and it would mean the world to me.

I really appreciate you taking the time to read and review this book.

Good luck
in your battles!!

I have more books for you!!

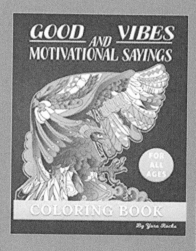

Made in the USA
Las Vegas, NV
07 November 2023

80383177R00046